The Scoop

Written by Mary-Anne Creasy

Illustrated by Omar Aranda

Flying Start
to Literacy®

Contents

Chapter 1

Hot off the press

"Get your latest *Crawford Crier* right here, hot off the press!"

Jackie waved a copy of the *Crawford Crier* at people passing by. She tucked a bundle of newspapers under her arm and paused at the grocery shop before entering.

Inside, she called out to Mr Kowalski. "Can I leave these newspapers here on the counter, please, Mr Kowalski?"

He turned his head and frowned. "I don't think so," he said. "They take up too much space on the counter. And last week, the wind blew them all over the floor and I had to pick them up." He looked down and continued unpacking boxes.

"Gee, thanks, Mr Kowalski," Jackie muttered. She trudged out of the shop.

"Mateo, wait up!" She spotted her friend in the distance. He was busy with his camera. He never went anywhere without his camera around his neck. Mateo stopped, spun around and lifted his camera. He snapped photos of Jackie as she walked towards him.

She put her hand in front of her face. "Don't take pictures of me. I'm the reporter. I'm not the story."

"Just practising, Jackie," said Mateo. "Did you get Mr Kowalski to take the newspapers?" He lowered the camera and began to check the images he had just taken.

"No, he's such a grump," said Jackie. "I don't think he likes me. And I don't think I like him."

"Forget about him. Let's interview the mayor for the Clock Festival story."

Jackie returned the newspapers to her backpack and grinned at Mateo. The pair made a good team. She wrote the stories and Mateo took the photos. They had talked about producing their own newspaper, and now that it was the summer holidays they were having fun doing all the things they imagined that real reporters and photographers did.

Near the town hall, Jackie spotted a white van parked up the road. "Look, it's the Channel 11 News van!" Jackie was wide-eyed. What a thrill! It could only mean one thing: her hero, TV news reporter Sylvia Da Luca, must be on location.

"I wonder what the story is," said Jackie. "Maybe Sylvia is doing a story on the Clock Festival, too. Let's see if we can find out."

She ran towards the van, breathless with excitement. Sylvia was flicking through the pages of a notebook. A cameraman packed equipment into the van.

"Excuse me, Ms Da Luca," Jackie said boldly. "I wanted to say hi. I watch you on TV all the time."

"Hi!" said Sylvia.

"I want to be a reporter just like you when I'm older."

Sylvia smiled. "Good for you. What's your name?"

"Jackie. I write the stories for our newspaper." She pulled a copy of the *Crawford Crier* out of her bag. "It's called the *Crawford Crier*. I like to write about the news in town. And this is Mateo. He takes all the photographs."

"I'm impressed," said Sylvia.

Jackie had an idea. "Can I interview you for our newspaper?"

"I'm not sure I have time." Sylvia hesitated. "I have to get back to the studio." She nodded at the cameraman who had finished packing up the van and was ready to go.

Jackie's face dropped. She looked so disappointed that Sylvia relented. "Okay, just one question," she said. "You'd better make it a good one."

Jackie knew exactly what she wanted to ask a star reporter like Sylvia. She pulled out a notebook, just like Sylvia's. "What do you think is the key to being a good reporter?"

"Well, there are news stories everywhere, Jackie. You just have to look for them. But the main thing is that you need to find an exciting angle for your story. Something that you think will interest people. Something to grab people's attention."

Jackie nodded and scribbled down Sylvia's advice. I know exactly what Sylvia means, she thought. And she was determined to find a story in her town and make it exciting, just like Sylvia would.

"And now I have to get back to work," said Sylvia. "Good luck with your newspaper."

Chapter 2

The big story in town

The mayor was a busy woman, but she had promised Jackie and Mateo an interview. She ushered the pair into her office.

The mayor began to recite some facts. "The history of the Clock Festival began when Albert Laredo, the famous clockmaker, moved to Crawford in 1924. Albert Laredo created his wonderful clocks because he loved the town. Each clock is unique and has an animal or magical creature theme. They are all over town so that everyone can enjoy them. Every year, the town celebrates these unique clocks with a festival. Tourists flock to our town to see the clocks and to enjoy the festivities."

The mayor took a deep breath and smiled as Mateo clicked his camera.

"This year the festival will be bigger and better than ever," she added, "because we've planned a surprise."

Jackie's eyes lit up. "Mayor, can you tell us what the surprise is? Or give us a clue?" If only Jackie could be first to find out what was planned. She might even be able to scoop Sylvia.

"Ha, ha!" The mayor shook her head. "No, but please mention the surprise to keep everyone guessing."

Afterwards, they stood on the front steps of the town hall and planned their next move.

"Let's take a photo of the fairy clock, first," suggested Mateo. The fairy clock was the most famous of the clocks. It had a huge face and a sculpture of fairies at its base. Some people said that a long time ago the fairies would spin when the clock struck the hour.

The fairy clock was on a pedestal in front of the library, near the town square. As Jackie and Mateo got close to the library, something seemed to be missing. The stone pedestal was empty. The plaque on the pedestal read "Fairy Clock, established 1924" but the fairy clock wasn't there.

Jackie frowned. "Where's the fairy clock?"

She looked around. Everybody in town was going about their business, as if the fairy clock was in its usual place. Nobody seemed to have noticed it was missing. What was wrong with people?

"Maybe it's being cleaned, in time for the festival," said Mateo. "Let's ask the librarian. Surely he'll know something."

RY CLOCK
TABLISHED
1924

The librarian shrugged. "I don't know anything about the fairy clock. Why don't you ask me about books? I'm a librarian. I know about books, not clocks."

"I think it's odd," Jackie said to Mateo. "The mayor didn't mention that one of the clocks was not in its usual place." Her imagination whirred into action. She sensed a story. "Take some photos, Mateo. We might have a scoop."

Jackie made notes. What kind of Clock Festival would it be if the fairy clock were missing? And who had taken it? What would you do with a big fairy clock? It would not be easy to hide, that's for sure. She thought about Sylvia's words. She needed an angle for her story. She needed to grab people's interest.

FAIRY CLOCK
ESTABLISHED
1924

Mateo took photos of the scene. He took close-ups of the empty pedestal, where the fairy clock should be. And he took other photos from a wide angle to get the whole library in the shot.

"Let's get photos of the other clocks," said Jackie.

"Yeah, we can't have a story about the Clock Festival without any photos of clocks," said Mateo. They headed towards the park, where there were more clocks on display.

15

Jackie and Mateo stared at the spot where the frog clock should be.

"Where are the clocks?" said Jackie, as Mateo took photos of the empty stone block. They raced to the other clocks. The lizard clock and the spider clock were gone, too!

Jackie screwed up her face. "What's going on?"

"Let's ask the park ranger," said Mateo. "Perhaps he'll know. He's in the park all day long."

"I don't know anything about the clocks," the park ranger shrugged. "Why don't you ask me about parks?"

Jackie frowned at Mateo. "There's something very weird going on here. I think it's pretty clear that the clocks have been stolen."

Then Mateo pointed at a pick-up truck. "Look!"

Over the road was a pick-up truck and on the back of the truck was a tarpaulin, which seemed to be covering a large, bulky object. Next to the truck was a man in an overcoat talking to Mr Kowalski.

"Who's that man with Mr Kowalski? I've never seen him, or that truck, in town before," said Jackie. "And what's in that truck?"

Mateo quickly took photos of the two men. He zoomed in to capture the men and the pick-up truck, before they made their getaway.

"I think I know what's under the tarpaulin," said Jackie. "Mr Kowalski and that man are stealing all the clocks! I think we have our story, Mateo!"

Chapter 3

Something's afoot!

The next day, Jackie and Mateo slowly rode their bikes past Mr Kowalski's shop. They were surprised to see a CLOSED sign hanging on the door. They stopped and pulled their bikes into the laneway next to the shop. Where was Mr Kowalski? Jackie thought. And why would he close his shop at this time of day?

"Let's take a look out the back," said Jackie. "Follow me."

The window at the back of the shop was high.

"We need to get a look in Mr Kowalski's shop," said Jackie, eyeing some empty crates in the laneway.

They dragged the empty crates under the window. Standing on the crates and on their tiptoes, they could peer into Mr Kowalski's darkened storeroom.

"Wow, what a mess," said Jackie. Boxes had been ripped open and stuff was scattered all over the floor. "Mr Kowalski doesn't keep his stock very neat, does he?"

Amid the mess, Mateo had noticed a large, lumpy object under a tarpaulin. "Look at that," he said. "Is that . . . ?"

"Oh, my," whispered Jackie excitedly. "That looks like the thing on the back of the pick-up truck!"

Then they heard a noise inside the storeroom and a flash of movement. Mateo quickly snapped photos. He was nervous. What if they got caught?

"Come on, let's get out of here," said Mateo. They leapt off the crates. Mateo shoved the camera into his backpack. They jumped on their bikes and cycled back to Mateo's house.

In the basement, Jackie wrote her story about the missing clocks, while Mateo uploaded the photos from his camera onto the computer. He scrolled through the photos to find the best ones. The photos from the storeroom were dark, so Mateo made them lighter.

"There's a lot of stuff in the photos," Mateo complained. "Even a weird shoe on the ground." He zoomed in on the covered object and then cropped everything else out.

"We should make this one of the photos in the story, and show the same tarpaulin we saw in the pick-up truck," he said. He looked at the photos of the pick-up truck and zoomed in on Mr Kowalski and the man in the overcoat.

"Let's turn on the news," said Jackie. "Maybe there's something about the missing clocks."

"Look," said Mateo, as Sylvia Da Luca appeared on the screen. "It's your hero."

Was she about to scoop them with a report on the missing clocks?

"Hey, look! She's at Mr Kowalski's shop!" said Jackie.

Sylvia was reporting from out the front of Mr Kowalski's shop.

"Here is a news flash," said Sylvia. "At Crawford this afternoon, there were a series of burglaries, including here at Mr Kowalski's grocery shop on Main Street. I'm sorry to report that we have a crime wave in our town! I wonder what Mr Kowalski thinks."

The camera showed Mr Kowalski.

"Mr Kowalski, what can you tell us about your burglary?" Sylvia shoved a microphone in front of his face.

"I closed my shop between three and four o'clock this afternoon and, while I was away, a burglar ransacked my storeroom and stole some valuable items of mine."

Jackie and Mateo gasped.

"Between three and four o'clock today," said Mateo.

"That's when we were there!" said Jackie.

"The police are urging anyone who might have been in the area," Sylvia went on, "or have seen something to please contact them."

"That's why the storeroom was such a mess. It was the burglar!" said Mateo. "Maybe there's a clue in the photos."

They hurried to check the photos on the computer. Mateo scrolled through them until he reached the storeroom ones. He zoomed in on one and moved the cursor around the image.

Jackie leant over his shoulder. "What are you looking for?" she asked.

"I'm not sure, but . . ." Then he saw the shoe.

"There, that shoe!" He pointed at the screen. "Doesn't that look weird?"

Jackie peered at the photo. "That's not just a shoe, that's a foot!" she said excitedly. "That must be the burglar!"

Mateo kept scrolling. "I think there might be more in other photos. Look at this photo. There's an outline of someone."

"There he is!" shouted Jackie, pointing at a shadowy figure. "Lighten that one!" When Mateo lightened the photo, the burglar's profile was visible.

"I think we've captured the burglar in these photos," said Mateo. "We should tell my mum."

Mateo's mum immediately called the police. Mateo emailed the photos to them.

Chapter 4

The surprising scoop

On the day of the Clock Festival, Jackie and Mateo had almost finished their newspaper article about the town's missing clocks and the culprits, Mr Kowalski and his friend. The article needed a few finishing touches, like a photo of the Clock Festival without any clocks! They hurried to the park.

A large crowd was gathered outside the library. People were exclaiming and cheering. They could hear a tinkling tune and children were clapping with excitement.

Jackie and Mateo pushed their way to the front of the crowd. And there, back in its place, was the fairy clock. The hour struck on the fairy clock, followed by loud chiming, and the fairies were spinning around its base.

"Hey, look at that!" said Mateo. And he took some photos.

They saw the mayor, beaming with pride. "What happened to your newspaper?" she asked Jackie. "I wanted to read about the Clock Festival."

Jackie lowered her head. "We thought the clocks were missing, stolen."

The mayor laughed. "No, they were being restored. Aren't they a wonderful surprise?"

"They're certainly a surprise," said Jackie.

"Yes, not the surprise we thought," said Mateo.

"What will we put in our newspaper now?" said Jackie. "We don't have a good story."

Jackie and Mateo followed the crowds further into the park. At the dog clock, they spotted Mr Kowalski and the man they didn't know. Mr Kowalski smiled and waved at them.

"Is that Mr Kowalski waving at us?" Jackie whispered to Mateo. "He's smiling, too."

"Yes, what's going on?" said Mateo. "He doesn't look grumpy and he's heading towards us, with that man."

"Jackie, Mateo," said Mr Kowalski. "I want to thank you. The police told me that it was your photos that helped them catch the burglar. He had stolen very precious things from my storeroom. They are not valuable, but they have belonged to my family for generations. And now I have them back."

He paused. "I'm not sure why you were snooping around my shop though!"

"We thought you were stealing the clocks," Jackie confessed. "I'm sorry. We saw you with this man and we thought we saw the clocks on the pick-up truck, but we were wrong."

Mr Kowalski glanced at the man. "I'd like you to meet someone."

"Allow me to introduce myself," the man said. "I am Anton Laredo. My grandfather was the creator of the clocks and I, too, am a clockmaker. Long ago, the clocks used to move and play music, but they got old and stopped working. So I collected them in my truck and fixed them for the festival."

"I was helping Anton move the clocks," added Mr Kowalski.

DOG CLOCK

The Channel 11 News van pulled up in the distance. Sylvia Da Luca, followed by the cameraman, dashed across the park in their direction.

"Jackie!" Sylvia said, a little out of breath. "I've been looking all over for you. I'm doing a story on camera."

"Are you here to do an interview with Anton Laredo?" asked Jackie.

Sylvia chuckled. "Stick around you two and you'll find out."

Jackie and Mateo watched and waited as Sylvia and the cameraman set up to do a story.

"Today is a big day for Crawford," announced Sylvia. "Not only is it the Clock Festival but also Crawford's crime wave is over! I've been informed that the alleged thief responsible for committing a series of burglaries has been charged by police."

"And the police have told me that we have to thank two local children, Jackie and Mateo. I can see them in the crowd. Come over here, you two!"

The pair looked at each other and grinned.

"Congratulations, Jackie and Mateo!" said Sylvia. The crowd cheered. "What do you have to say?"

"Don't forget to get a copy of the *Crawford Crier* everyone!" said Jackie. "Hot off the press tomorrow." She winked at Mateo. "Our next edition will be our own story. How we helped to catch a burglar. We got the scoop!"

A note from the author

News stories have always been valuable sources of information. Before TV or the Internet, a newspaper that got a scoop – that broke a story first – would likely sell many more newspapers than any other newspaper. Often, visual images such as photographs help back up a story and they also attract readers' attention.

In this story, I wanted to show that sometimes what you see might not be the truth. A photograph can easily be misunderstood. A photograph can be cropped to leave something out. It can be taken at an angle that makes the subject look bigger or smaller.

Luckily, Mateo was so enthusiastic about taking photos constantly that he took the one photo that solved the real crime in the town and gave the *Crawford Crier* the scoop.